REWRITE YOUR NORMAL

A WORKBOOK FOR REBELS, SURVIVORS, AND CYCLE-BREAKERS

LISA GERARDY

Welcome!

If you're holding this workbook, it means something brave already happened:

- You chose to turn inward instead of away.
- You chose curiosity over silence.
- You chose your voice, even if it still shakes a little.

This isn't a workbook about becoming "better." It's about becoming truer. Inside these pages, you'll write. You'll remember. You'll unlearn.

There are no right answers here. No grades. No gold stars for perfection. Only space. Space to reflect, to question, to speak on paper what once felt unspeakable.

You belong here. Take your time. Track your truth. Take the pen back. The story is yours now, and I'm honored to walk these pages with you.

Lisa Gerardy

ABOUT ME

I'm Lisa Gerardy, the author of Chasing Normal, a memoir about surviving childhood trauma, choosing healing, and rewriting my life on my own terms. I teach writing, speak about breaking cycles, and believe that humor and honesty can absolutely coexist, especially when we're telling the hardest truths.

How to Use This Workbook

Rewrite Your Normal is designed to help you slow down, reflect, and create new patterns that support the life you want.

- Start where you are – You do not need to have read Chasing Normal to use this workbook. Each section stands on its own and guides you step by step. There are no page numbers to follow. Start wherever you want.

- Make space for honesty – Your story deserves clarity. Use these prompts to explore what shaped you, what protected you, and what no longer serves you. Be truthful in a way that feels safe and grounded.

- Write freely and without judgment – Let your thoughts flow. These pages are for you and no one else. The goal is expression, not perfection.

- Take breaks when needed – Some exercises may bring up strong emotions. Pause whenever you need to breathe, reflect, or step away. You are allowed to move slowly. You are allowed to return later.

- Use the prompts more than once – As you grow, your answers may change. Revisit sections when you feel stuck, curious, or ready for a deeper layer of insight.

- Bring this work into conversations – Use these pages with a therapist, support group, book club, or trusted friend. Connection can strengthen healing.

- Celebrate your progress – You are rewriting patterns that may have been in place for generations. Every page you complete is evidence of your courage and commitment to yourself.

This is your space to explore, release, and rebuild.
Take your time. Your story is unfolding with intention now.

We Don't Talk About That

Theme: Silence, Secrets, and Shame

Silence became a language I learned long before I ever learned to write. My earliest memories aren't of toys, birthdays, or bedtime stories. They're of the unspoken rules that lived in the walls of my grandmother's house in Peoria, IL, where I was first abused at age two. I was taught to hold my breath, hold my words, and hold the truth inside my body like a secret I never agreed to carry. Love and danger lived side-by-side, and the rule was simple: we don't talk about that.

When I tried to speak about what my uncle was doing to me, I was shut down. When I asked questions, I was redirected. When I told the truth, I was taught to change the story. Over time, silence didn't just protect the family; it shaped me. It became my survival strategy, my shame, and my shadow. Breaking that silence as an adult wasn't just a choice; it was an act of rebellion, recovery, and reclamation of my voice.

Healing began the moment I understood that silence wasn't protection. It was imprisonment. Speaking, first in whispers, then in writing, and finally out loud, became how I broke the generational rule: we don't talk about that.

Now, it's your turn to end your silence. The next few pages are yours to use as you see fit. You don't have to share with anyone unless you want to.

UNPACK

What role did silence play in your family growing up?

_____

_____

_____

_____

What messages taught you not to speak up?

_____

_____

_____

_____

TAKE CONTROL

Finish this sentence:

The thing I was never allowed to talk about was...

_____

_____

_____

_____

Now rewrite the rule:

In my life today, I give myself permission to...

_____

_____

_____

_____

WRITE IT OUT

- If I had been allowed to tell the truth back then...
- What I needed most was someone who would have...

Chosen Family

Theme: Reclaiming Connection

In 1974, when I was three, I learned that there were people outside of my family who cared about me. I found comfort not from blood relatives, but from kind neighbors who became my first chosen family. People like Fran and Laura offered what I didn't even know I needed—gentle consistency, warmth, and affection without fear. Their homes smelled of cigarettes, cookies, and cats. These are smells I still associate with peace and calm. They didn't rescue me from my life, but they gave me a place to rest inside it.

Those visits were small, quiet interruptions from the fear and anxiety I lived with at home. They planted something that would outlive the abuse: the belief that love could be soft, safe, and freely given. Looking back, I understand that I wasn't just escaping my house; I was discovering a truth that would save me later. I learned I could do better when I was an adult someday. It gave me hope and a map to "normalcy."

"Aunt" Fran, "Grandma" Laura, and "Cousin" Nicole taught me that family isn't only blood. Sometimes, it's the people who choose you when you've never been chosen before.

Think about your own chosen family. If you choose, answer any, all, or none of the questions on the pages that follow this.

UNPACK

Who were the people in your childhood who made you feel safe, seen, or understood—even briefly?

_____

_____

_____

_____

What did you learn about love or safety from those relationships?

_____

_____

_____

_____

TAKE CONTROL

Finish this sentence:

Family, to me, used to mean...

Now rewrite the rule:

The kind of family I am choosing to build today is...

WRITE IT OUT

- The people who felt like home to me were…
- Family was something I was born into, but now I know…

Crayons and Jesus

Theme: Early Beliefs and Control

I began kindergarten at age four at the local Lutheran school. At St. Mark's, I discovered how to color inside the lines, literally with crayons, and emotionally with obedience. I tried to fit into the quiet order of the classroom and the strict order of religion, but I always felt a little off-tempo, like I was humming a different song than everyone else. Mom and I were not members of the church like the other families.

Some kids carried confidence as easily as I carried stomachaches. I watched them glide through the day while I tried to stay out of trouble, out of sight, and free of my mother's voice, which followed me even when she wasn't there. Still, there were flickers of hope, like the day I was brave enough to recite the alphabet aloud. I loved skipping out to "aunt" Fran's gray Barracuda after school and going to her duplex, where I felt safe.

Even though I never got into the religious aspect of St. Marks, I really liked my friends and the peaceful atmosphere. Unfortunately, halfway through first grade, Mom could no longer afford the tuition. She refused a scholarship based on joining the church. So, off to the Broward County Public School system I went. It was a lot louder, but at least I didn't have to memorize Bible verses.

UNPACK

What were the earliest rules you learned about being "good" or "acceptable"?

_____

_____

_____

_____

Did school, church, or another early environment shape your beliefs about yourself? How?

_____

_____

_____

_____

TAKE CONTROL

Finish this sentence:

As a child, I believed that being good meant...

_____

_____

_____

_____

Now rewrite the rule:

Now I believe...

_____

_____

_____

_____

WRITE IT OUT

- I learned early that approval was earned by…
- The first time I felt out of place, I remember…

Stomachaches and Bad Grades

Theme: The Body Remembers

By the time I was seven, my body had already begun telling the truth my mouth wasn't allowed to speak. I learned early that love could turn into anger in seconds, and my nervous system stayed on alert like a watchguard that never slept. My grades slipped not because I didn't understand the work, but because fear took up more space in my brain than multiplication or spelling ever could. Every red mark on a report card felt like a flare, proof that I was failing at being both a student and a child worth loving.

My stomachaches became my first symptom of anxiety. While other kids brought home gold stars and crayon drawings, I brought home tight muscles, sleeplessness, and gastrointestinal distress. At home, the tension lived in the walls, and I learned to read my mother's tone for clues, for danger, for survival.

Trying to be perfect became my safety plan. If I just behaved, achieved, or disappeared, maybe I could keep the storm from starting. It never worked, but it taught me something powerful. Children are not dramatic, broken, or difficult. They are responding to the world they're raised in, and their bodies keep the score long before the report cards do.

UNPACK

What early physical symptoms did you experience that you now recognize as emotional responses?

_____

_____

_____

_____

How did the adults in your life interpret your distress? (Concern, anger, dismissal, avoidance?)

_____

_____

_____

_____

TAKE CONTROL

Finish this sentence:

My body tried to warn me by...

_____

....

....

....

Now rewrite the rule:

Now I honor those signals by...

_____

....

....

_____

WRITE IT OUT

- My body knew the truth before I did…
- The illness, anxiety, or behavior was really…

Secret Eating and Kiddie City

Theme: Shame and Survival

By 1980, food had become comfort, rebellion, and my first quiet attempt at self-soothing. When I was home alone after school, and the apartment settled into silence and no one was watching, I slipped into the kitchen like a ghost, filling the ache inside me with cold chicken legs, spoonfuls of cookie dough, or whatever leftover scraps I could find. I was eating to comfort myself because I could not rely on my mother for soothing. I didn't know then that the craving wasn't for sugar or salt, but for peace, safety, and control over even one small part of my life.

In the summer, Mom sent me to Kiddie City. This is where I got flashes of normal childhood with the sticky popsicles, and sweaty summer air, but even in that chaos, I still felt like I was performing childhood instead of living it. I learned how to blend in, how to laugh on cue, how to be the funny kid instead of the hurting one. Meanwhile, food became the language my body used when I didn't have permission to say: I'm lonely. I'm scared. I need something chewy and delicious.

This wasn't gluttony. It was strategy. I was a child finding a way to survive the emotional famine she couldn't name.

UNPACK

What did you use as comfort when emotional needs weren't being met?

_____

_____

_____

_____

What feelings were you trying to soothe, avoid, or numb?

_____

_____

_____

_____

TAKE CONTROL

Finish this sentence:

What I was really hungry for was...

_____

_____

_____

_____

Now rewrite the rule:

Today, I honor that need by...

_____

_____

_____

_____

WRITE IT OUT

- **I didn't need food—I needed…**
- **No one saw how hard I was trying to survive, but…**

Orange Trees and Miss Kitty

Theme: Safe Love and Nonjudgmental Connection

In the middle of all the noise and chaos, there was Miss Kitty, the first being who loved me without conditions, expectations, or moods I had to manage. She was steady warmth in a world that was anything but. I remember sitting under the orange trees in the backyard, breathing in their sweet scent, my back against the rough bark, Miss Kitty curled in my lap like a small, breathing shield. For a few borrowed minutes at a time, the world softened. No yelling. No rules. No pretending. Just purring and citrus air and the feeling of being allowed to exist.

Miss Kitty and I had found each other in the overgrown back yard of the Taylor Street duplex. She was the only stray to let me pet her, so I let her follow me into the apartment one day, after school, before my mom got home.

I loved Miss Kitty. She didn't care about grades, weight, behavior, or whether I'd kept the peace in the house. She didn't tell me I was too emotional, too dramatic, too much. She just stayed. That cat was the first one to teach me that love didn't have to hurt or shout to be real. That safe connection wasn't a fantasy—it was possible. Even now, when I think of peace, I don't picture a church, a classroom, or a person. I picture an orange tree and a purring cat.

UNPACK

Did you have an animal, toy, object, or place that made you feel safe as a child?

_____

_____

_____

_____

What did that connection teach you—about love, about comfort, about being seen?

_____

_____

_____

_____

TAKE CONTROL

Finish this sentence:

I learned from that animal/place/thing that love can be…

_____

_____

_____

_____

Now rewrite the rule:

I now allow love into my life that feels…

_____

_____

_____

_____

WRITE IT OUT

- The first time I truly felt safe was when...
- Someone in my life didn't ask me to prove my worth...

Prime Rib Breakfasts and Rubik's Cube Dreams

Theme: Chaos Mixed with Moments of Magic

When I was a ten, some of the gentlest moments in my life didn't happen at home. One of them was during a sleepover at a summer camp friend's house. Her parents had gone on a date the night before so we dipped into the leftover prime rib for breakfast. It felt extravagant and strange in the best way. I was used to instant oatmeal or cereal.

More than the food, it was the kindness that stayed with me. Her mom noticed me. She remembered my birthday and gave me a Rubik's Cube and a stuffed koala. These may seem like small gifts, but they are huge when you're a child who isn't used to being seen.

The Rubik's Cube became a quiet obsession. I was convinced that if I could just turn the pieces the right way, everything would line up and make sense. I didn't yet understand that some things aren't puzzles to be solved; they're environments you're meant to leave. But those moments mattered. They showed me that warmth, attention, and steadiness existed somewhere in the world, even if I didn't live there yet.

UNPACK

Did you ever feel like you were trying to make sense of adults' choices as a child? What did that feel like?

_____

_____

_____

_____

What were the small moments of joy, wonder, or escape that helped you cope?

_____

_____

_____

_____

TAKE CONTROL

Finish this sentence:

I used to believe that if I tried hard enough, I could fix...

_____

_____

_____

_____

Now rewrite the rule:

Now I know that some things were never mine to fix...

_____

_____

_____

_____

WRITE IT OUT

- I tried to solve my life like a puzzle when really…
- The magic I remember from childhood was…

Fifth Grade Spy

Theme: Parentification — Being the Adult Too Soon

Fifth grade was the year I learned that adults could turn children into spies. My mom asked me to secretly record a conversation she had with the local Ford dealer. I became a one-person surveillance team with a tape recorder hidden in a "purse."

With a big stomachache, I sat in the man's office on a hard plastic chair. I was so nervous, but I wanted to do a good job for my mom. I didn't want her to get angry at me if I messed up. So, I held the tape recorder, hidden in a blue vinyl bank bag, and tried to act like it was just a normal thing that kids do.

I thought I was being helpful, even loyal, but underneath it all was a quieter truth: I was being asked to carry weight no child should ever have to hold. What looked like "maturity" from the outside was really vigilance, and what looked like responsibility was really survival.

That year, I began to confuse closeness with caretaking, love with labor, and safety with control. I didn't know then that real love never requires a child to be the adult in the room.

UNPACK

Were you ever expected to keep secrets, manage emotions, or protect adults when you were young?

_____

_____

_____

_____

How has this shaped your adult relationships today?

_____

_____

_____

_____

TAKE CONTROL

Finish this sentence:

I was taught that love meant taking care of other people's feelings, but now I know...

_____

_____

_____

_____

Now rewrite the rule:

As an adult, I give myself permission to...

_____

_____

_____

_____

WRITE IT OUT

- I was a child with an adult job...
- I didn't know I was being trained, I just thought...

Yellow on the Fourth of July

Theme: Powerlessness and Resilience

I was ten years old, and while other kids were running barefoot through sprinklers and chasing fireflies, I was in the hospital with excruciating abdominal pain. It took a while for the doctors to figure out what was wrong. Hepatitis, they eventually said, after days of tests and words I didn't yet understand but could feel in my body. I learned quickly how long nights could be,

It was the Fourth of July. The world outside exploded in color, fireworks lighting up the sky, and I watched them through a hospital window while my insides rebelled. I felt dim and distant, like I was watching life from behind glass, close enough to see but too far away to touch. Somewhere beyond that window, kids laughed and shouted, parents called them in for popsicles, and summer kept going without me. From my bed, the booms sounded muffled, like even the celebration knew it wasn't meant for me.

Still, even in the fear and the medical words I couldn't translate, there were small bursts of something real. The other patients' mothers helped to calm me when my own mother could not. They rubbed my back, explained procedures in softer voices, and stayed when my mom had to work. In a room full of uncertainty, their kindness was steady, and it taught me something I would carry with me: sometimes the people who show up for you are not the ones you expect, but they matter just as much.

UNPACK

What did illness or injury teach you about your body, safety, or worth as a child?

_____

_____

_____

_____

Were you given information or left in the dark?

_____

_____

_____

_____

TAKE CONTROL

Finish this sentence:

As a child, I thought being sick meant I was weak, but now I know...

_____

_____

_____

_____

Now rewrite the rule:

I honor my body now by...

_____

_____

_____

_____

WRITE IT OUT

- **The first time I felt powerless, I remember…**
- **When I was sick, what I needed was…**

Dull, Not Shiny

Theme: Comparisons and Worth

When I started middle school, I started noticing how other kids lived and how different my life looked in comparison. Their homes were tidy, their bikes were new, and their clothes matched instead of being "close enough." Even in sixth-grade band, I stood out. Everyone else showed up with shiny rented instruments, while my clarinet was dull and scuffed, clearly not new. My mom had attempted suicide the evening we were supposed to go to school to rent an instrument, so I played what we could afford. I didn't know the word envy yet, but I felt the sting of being outside the glow. Everything about them seemed polished. Everything about me felt worn, borrowed, or quietly explained away.

I also didn't know then that what I carried was not failure. It was resilience. I learned to live inside instability. My mom's moods, her relationships, her paycheck, her storms. I learned to adjust myself instead of expecting the world to adjust for me. Shame came early, but so did a strange kind of pride. I could function without the things other kids seemed to need to feel secure or special.

That chapter was the beginning of a lifelong lesson. Having less did not mean being less. The shine I thought I was missing was not in new instruments or matching outfits. It was in endurance, adaptability, and the scrappy kind of hope that grows even in low light conditions.

UNPACK

How did you judge yourself as a child—appearance, money, family, belongings, grades, etc.?

_____

_____

_____

_____

How did you learn to adapt, blend in, or hide what you didn't have?

_____

_____

_____

_____

TAKE CONTROL

Finish this sentence:

I used to believe that having more meant being more, but now I know...

_____

_____

_____

_____

Now rewrite the rule:

The truth about my worth is...

_____

_____

_____

_____

WRITE IT OUT

- I thought everyone else had it better, but really…
- The part of me that survived without was…

Open Psych

Theme: Chaos, Fear, and the Illusion of Control

I was only eleven when I learned that adults could break. It was after my mother's second suicide attempt, and I learned just as quickly that children could be left holding the pieces. When my mom's pain became too big to hide, the world shifted. There were hospital visits, whispered phone calls, and a kind of silence that was not calm but charged. I saw how quickly a parent could disappear behind a locked door marked Psych, and how love did not always protect someone from themselves.

I did not understand mental illness then. I did not have language for trauma, depression, or suicidal ideation. I only knew that something terrifying was happening and that no one was saying it out loud. Even as a child, I began trying to manage the emotional temperature around me, as if staying calm could keep her alive. That was my first experience of trying to control the uncontrollable.

Looking back, that chapter became the beginning of a vow I never spoke but carried in my bones. If pain could be passed down, then someone in the family had to be the one to stop it. I did not know the phrase cycle breaker yet, but I was already becoming one.

UNPACK

Were you ever exposed to an adult's mental illness, instability, or emotional collapse as a child?

_____

_____

_____

_____

Did you ever try to fix, calm, or emotionally manage an adult? How did that affect you later?

_____

_____

_____

_____

TAKE CONTROL

Finish this sentence:

I thought it was my job to hold everything together...

_____

_____

_____

_____

Now rewrite the rule:

The truth is...

_____

_____

_____

_____

WRITE IT OUT

- I learned that love doesn't always save someone...
- I realized my parent was not invincible was when...

Hiding from Rod

Theme: Fear and Safety Instincts

It was New Year's 1982. My mother had been with her abusive boyfriend, Rod, for four years by then, and fear had become part of the air I breathed. That night, they dropped me off at an all-night daycare. Sometime in the middle of the night, Rod showed up alone and tried to pick me up. I remember pulling the thin blanket over my head and hiding on my cot, holding my breath and willing myself to disappear. Even at that age, I understood something was wrong, even if no one explained it to me.

My mom's relationship with Rod taught me how quickly safety could turn into danger, how a single footstep or a slammed door could change the atmosphere of an entire house. I learned to move quietly, to listen before I walked, to read faces and voices the way other kids read clocks. I did not call it survival back then. I just called it being careful.

What I did not know yet was that I was already developing instincts that would stay with me for decades. Hypervigilance. Emotional scanning. A body that never fully relaxed. But even in the fear, there was something else beginning to grow. A small, stubborn voice inside me whispered, You will not live like this forever. I did not have words like boundaries or a safety plan, but I had a seed of resistance, and sometimes that was enough to keep me going.

UNPACK

What did fear look or feel like in your childhood home?

_____

_____

_____

_____

How did you learn to sense danger before it arrived? What were your early warning signs?

_____

_____

_____

_____

TAKE CONTROL

Finish this sentence:

I thought fear meant I was weak, but now I know…

_____

_____

_____

_____

Now rewrite the rule:

Today, I listen to my body's signals by…

_____

_____

_____

_____

WRITE IT OUT

- I learned to walk quietly because...
- My body knew when I wasn't safe, because...

Merry #@$% Christmas!

Theme: Holidays and Broken Illusions

When I was twelve, my mother flung our cheap fake Christmas tree across the room and yelled, "Merry effing Christmas." That was the moment I learned that holidays don't fix anything. They just decorate the damage. Christmas in my house wasn't cocoa and comfort. It was a pressure cooker wrapped in tinsel. The tree looked fine from the outside, the lights sparkled, and the presents sat under the branches like props in a play. Underneath it all lived tension, shouting, slammed doors, and the kind of silence that hurt more than noise.

I tried hard to believe in the Christmas magic I saw in movies, the kind where families gather and love wins by the final scene. I wanted that version so badly. But every attempt at normal in our house fell apart before dessert. Pretending became part of the ritual, and I learned early that some of the most broken days are the ones that are supposed to feel whole.

Still, the lights stayed on. They glowed in the window even when nothing else felt bright. That stayed with me. Beauty and pain can share the same room. Wonder can survive even when joy doesn't. And somewhere in all of that mess, a quieter part of me was already learning how to find the flicker in the dark.

UNPACK

Were you ever asked to "act happy" or pretend things were fine? How did that affect you?

_____

_____

_____

_____

What small moments of real joy or beauty do you remember from those chaotic holidays?

_____

_____

_____

_____

TAKE CONTROL

Finish this sentence:

I believed holidays had to feel perfect, but now I know...

_____

_____

_____

_____

Now rewrite the rule:

The way I choose to celebrate now is...

_____

_____

_____

_____

WRITE IT OUT

- The lights were brighter than the people in the room…
- If I could rewrite one holiday memory, I would choose…

Imposter Syndrome and School

Theme: Belonging, Achievement, and Self-Doubt

In seventh grade, I was asked to take the SAT for Duke University's talent program. Instead of feeling proud, I panicked. I threw the paperwork away. I was terrified that if I did badly, my mom would be angry, and I had already learned that disappointing her felt dangerous. It was easier to pretend the opportunity never existed than to risk failing out loud.

School was supposed to be the place where effort earned reward, where learning built confidence, where teachers noticed the quiet kid doing her best. I worked twice as hard just to feel halfway enough, always waiting for someone to tap me on the shoulder and say, "Sorry, there's been a mistake. You don't actually belong here."

Even when I succeeded, I didn't trust it. Good grades felt like accidents. Praise felt like a setup. Confidence seemed like something other kids were born with and I had somehow missed. I didn't know the term imposter syndrome yet, but I lived inside it. Every A felt temporary. Every accomplishment felt borrowed. I was always bracing for the moment someone would figure out I wasn't who they thought I was.

What I didn't understand then was that self doubt isn't proof of inadequacy. It is a scar from growing up in a world where praise was rare, safety was inconsistent, and worth had to be earned instead of assumed.

UNPACK

When was the first time you remember feeling "not good enough," even when you were trying your best?

_____

_____

_____

_____

Did you ever feel like you were pretending to belong — in school, friendships, family, religion, etc.?

_____

_____

_____

_____

TAKE CONTROL

Finish this sentence:

I used to believe I had to prove my worth through performance, but now I know...

_____

_____

_____

_____

Now rewrite the rule:

What I offer the world that has nothing to do with achievement is...

_____

_____

_____

_____

WRITE IT OUT

- They thought I was confident, but really…
- I wasn't afraid of failing; I was afraid of being seen…

The Great Escape

Theme: Achievement as Armor

After seventh grade, I learned that escape does not always look like running away. Sometimes it looks like being transferred. Leaving McNichol Middle School was not just a change in buildings. It was a shift in atmosphere, identity, and possibility. A school boundary rule moved me to Olsen, and what could have been a small bureaucratic detail became a lifeline. For the first time, I was not trapped in a place where I did not belong. I was suddenly somewhere new, somewhere lighter, somewhere filled with people who did not know who I had been, which meant I could become someone different.

At Olsen, I met Hillary and other friends who shaped my sense of belonging in ways school never had before. I learned that achievement could be more than survival. It could be a doorway. I could use good grades, humor, effort, and personality not just as protection, but as access. Leaving one school was not just an exit. It was an opening into a version of myself that finally had room to breathe.

That was the beginning of understanding that sometimes the system breaks in your favor. And even when you do not have control, you might still have momentum.

UNPACK

Have you ever experienced a shift in environment (school, home, friends) that changed how you saw yourself?

_____

_____

_____

_____

Did you ever use achievement, humor, perfection, or performance as a way to feel safe or accepted?

_____

_____

_____

_____

TAKE CONTROL

Finish this sentence:

I believed I had to prove myself to belong, but now I know...

_____

_____

_____

_____

Now rewrite the rule:

The truth is...

_____

_____

_____

_____

WRITE IT OUT

- I didn't know it then, but moving helped me by...
- The first time I felt like I could reinvent myself was...

Codeine in the Girls' Room

Theme: Adultification and Neglect

When I was in middle school, my mother stole liquid Tylenol with codeine from her job. When I asked to stay home with menstrual cramps, she shoved a small bottle of red liquid at me and told me to put it in my purse and take a swig or two in the bathroom at school when I needed it.

I was still a kid when I learned what codeine tasted like. Not because a doctor prescribed it, but because the one adult in my life treated medication like a shortcut for silence. Pain, anxiety, exhaustion, it did not matter what the problem was. The answer was always the same. Here, take this. Not care. Not comfort. Just chemicals and compliance.

I took liquid opiates in school bathrooms while other girls shared lip gloss and secrets. That was the beginning of my adultification. I was expected to cope with adult solutions to problems I never should have had. No one asked what I was feeling. They just wanted me quiet, manageable, and out of the way.

Looking back, I see it clearly now. I was not being cared for. I was being managed. Neglect is not always empty refrigerators or absent adults. Sometimes it is a bottle of liquid medicine and a child who slowly stops believing she deserves tenderness.

UNPACK

Were you ever given responsibilities, information, or burdens that were too heavy for your age?

_____

....

....

....

_____

Did caregivers use substances, silence, or dismissal instead of support? How did that affect you?

_____

....

....

....

_____

TAKE CONTROL

Finish this sentence:

I thought growing up fast made me strong, but now I know…

_____

_____

_____

_____

Now rewrite the rule:

My younger self deserved…

_____

_____

_____

_____

WRITE IT OUT

- I didn't need medicine, I needed…
- They called it helping, but really they were avoiding…

Losing a Father, Gaining a Dad

Theme: Grief and Complicated Love

From 1984 to 1986, I learned that fatherhood and biology are not the same thing. During that time, my mom met my stepdad by the pool of our apartment building. He was twenty years older than her, an Italian guy from Boston, and a World War II veteran. I spent a lot of time nearby, listening more than speaking, trying to understand a life that still felt like it was happening to me instead of with me.

Then came 1986, the year my biological father died. His absence had always been louder than his presence, but death made it permanent. I felt grief and relief at the same time, and I did not know that was allowed. I was not just mourning a man. I was mourning the fantasy that he might someday show up and become the father I needed. Losing him forced me to confront one of the hardest truths of my life. You cannot heal a wound by waiting for someone to love you the way they should have in the first place.

And yet, in that loss, something opened. There was space for the possibility of another kind of father figure, one chosen rather than inherited. This was the start of learning that family is bigger than DNA, that closure is not always forgiveness, and that the love we deserve may not come from the people who gave us life, but it may still come.

UNPACK

Did you ever grieve someone who wasn't really there for you — a parent, friend, partner, or mentor?

_____

_____

_____

_____

Have you ever found healing or wisdom from an unexpected person or place? What did it teach you?

_____

_____

_____

_____

TAKE CONTROL

Finish this sentence:

I used to believe love had to come from the people I was
born to, but now I know...

_____

_____

_____

_____

Now rewrite the rule:

A truth I'm learning about family is...

_____

_____

_____

_____

WRITE IT OUT

- I confused being abandoned with being unworthy…
- The kind of father I needed was…

Young Love

Theme: Naivety and First Attachment

Dating Will taught me how actions can disguise themselves as love. He was two years younger than me, but he was very much in charge. From the outside, it looked intense and grown up. From the inside, it was confusing, consuming, and quietly damaging. Our relationship was highly sexual and emotionally volatile, and I mistook that intensity for connection.

Will was verbally abusive in ways I did not yet have language for. He called me a whore. He told me I should be punished for having had sex before I met him, as if my past made me permanently guilty. I learned to absorb shame that did not belong to me, to apologize for things I did not do wrong, and to confuse control with care.

I believed that if I could just be better, quieter, more acceptable, the relationship would stabilize. I did not know then that what I was calling chemistry was actually familiarity. It felt normal because it echoed the emotional terrain I already knew.

I did not know how much that relationship would shape me until much later. I learned that validation borrowed from someone else never lasts, and that love rooted in shame is not love at all. I could not heal through someone else's approval. That work would eventually have to start with the girl looking back at me in the mirror.

UNPACK

Who was your first "big" attachment—the one that felt like a beginning, even if it was breaking you?

_____

_____

_____

_____

What parts of yourself did you shrink, soften, hide, or abandon in order to stay in that relationship?

_____

_____

_____

_____

TAKE CONTROL

Finish this sentence:

I thought love meant holding on, but now I know...

_____

....

....

....

Now rewrite the rule:

The version of me who loved too hard deserved...

_____

....

....

....

WRITE IT OUT

- I thought we were soulmates, but really we were…
- What I wanted from him was really…

One of These Afternoons

Theme: Boundary Confusion and Early Sexualization

My sophomore year was when I started learning the difference between wanting attention and wanting ownership of my own body. RJ and I spent those afternoons wrapped in hormones and soundtrack choices, The Eagles' Greatest Hits on repeat, and a kind of closeness that felt grown up even though neither of us really was.

I wanted to say yes. I wanted to feel chosen. But I also knew what happened to girls who said yes without protection. I had already seen too much of what teen motherhood looked like by observing my mother's relationship with my older brother.

So I said no because some part of me was already trying to save my future self. I did not have the words consent, body autonomy, or trauma repetition yet, but I had instinct. Something in me knew that desire did not require surrender. That caution was not weakness. That I did not owe my body just because someone wanted it.

That time in my life was the beginning of understanding that boundaries do not just protect. They define us. And even the quietest no can be an act of self-love. If only that lesson stuck with me into adulthood.

UNPACK

When was the first time you felt pressured to give more than you were ready to?

_____

_____

_____

_____

What beliefs did you internalize about desire, morals, shame, or responsibility?

_____

_____

_____

_____

TAKE CONTROL

Finish this sentence:

I thought boundaries were rejection, but now I know...

_____

....

....

....

_____

Now rewrite the rule:

Today, allow myself to...

_____

....

....

....

_____

WRITE IT OUT

- I wanted to, but I said no because…
- I was already learning how to protect myself…

The Magic of Alcohol

Theme: Escape and Illusion

I discovered wine coolers during my Freshman year of high school. Alcohol stopped being something adults did in the next room and became something I used to survive the one I was in. It slid into my life like a magician—flashy, distracting, full of promise. For a while, it worked. One drink and the world softened. The memories blurred. The noise inside me went quiet. I thought I had found freedom, but really, I had found a pause button.

I didn't understand yet that numbness is not the same thing as peace. Alcohol helped me avoid feelings I didn't have the skills to process, and for a while, that felt like relief. But illusion always fades. I began to realize that the pain I thought I had escaped was still waiting for me, just quieter, just patient. Drinking was simply postponing what eventually demanded to be felt.

This chapter of my life marks the beginning of a lifelong truth: coping mechanisms can be both life preservers and anchors. They keep us afloat until they start pulling us under. Like all habits, alcohol started affecting my health.

UNPACK

What was the first thing you used to cope, escape, or numb?

_____

....

....

....

_____

What did you think it was giving you at the time? What was it actually taking?

_____

....

....

....

_____

TAKE CONTROL

Finish this sentence:

I thought avoiding pain was the same as recovering from it, but now I know…

_____

_____

_____

_____

Now rewrite the rule:

Today, I allow myself to feel because…

_____

_____

_____

_____

WRITE IT OUT

- Alcohol felt like a shortcut to freedom, but really…
- The first time I drank, I was trying to quiet…

Being Pimped for Weed

Theme: Betrayal and Exploitation

The summer after my sophomore year of high school, I got back in touch with a girl I'd known in elementary school. I wouldn't really call her a friend, though. She'd sat next to me once. That was about it. But she reappeared like we had history, like she'd always been on my side.

She made it seem like I was being included in something special, like I'd finally been invited inside a world I'd been standing outside of for a long time. What I didn't realize was that she wasn't offering me belonging. She was using me.

She wanted marijuana from a boy she knew. And to get it, she offered him me. That day, my body became a bargaining chip. Not for anything I wanted. Not for my benefit. Just something she could spend to get what she wanted.

From the outside, it probably looked like I went along with it. That's how these stories often get told. But inside, it didn't feel like choice or rebellion or consent. It felt like freezing. Like doing what was expected because no one had ever explained that I was allowed to expect better. Or say no. Or leave.

Afterward, the shame landed exactly where it always seems to land. On me. She walked away untouched, and I carried it like I'd done something wrong just by being there.

UNPACK

Have you ever been pressured or coerced into anything that looked like a choice but didn't feel like one?

_____

_____

_____

_____

What messages did you internalize about your worth, your voice, or your right to refuse?

_____

_____

_____

_____

TAKE CONTROL

Finish this sentence:

I thought what happened was my fault, but now I know…

_____

_____

_____

_____

Now rewrite the rule:

The truth is…

_____

_____

_____

_____

WRITE IT OUT

- They used my need for belonging against me...
- I wasn't choosing; I was surviving...

Nice Guy Rebound

Theme: Settling for Safety

After Will's abuse, I needed someone kind. Ed was older, stable, and predictable. He was the boyfriend I thought I should want after the chaos I'd survived. He sent me care packages when I was away at FSU, showed up when he said he would, and didn't make me guess whether I mattered. That should have brought comfort, but instead, it brought confusion.

I didn't know how to receive care without suspicion. I didn't know how to stay when someone wasn't hurting me. I didn't know how to exist in a relationship where I didn't have to prove myself every second just to be tolerated. So instead of softening, I resisted. I pushed. I tested. I treated him poorly and didn't understand why until years later: kindness felt unsafe because I didn't yet feel worthy of it.

My years with Ed taught me something I wasn't ready to say out loud: safety without emotional intimacy can still feel empty, and a "nice guy" can't fill the space that unhealed wounds leave inside you. Love wasn't the problem; readiness was. I didn't need someone better. I needed to become someone who believed she deserved love without earning it first.

UNPACK

Have you ever sabotaged a healthy relationship because it felt "too good"?

_____

_____

_____

_____

What do you now understand about the difference between safety, settling, and true connection?

_____

_____

_____

_____

TAKE CONTROL

Finish this sentence:

I thought someone else could heal me by loving me, but now I know...

_____

_____

_____

_____

Now rewrite the rule:

The version of me who didn't know how to receive love needed...

_____

_____

_____

_____

WRITE IT OUT

- I didn't know how to stay when someone was gentle...
- Kindness felt dangerous because...

Group Therapy

Theme: Vulnerability and Shared Healing

Walking into that group therapy room felt like stepping into a spotlight and a hiding place at the same time; exposed and invisible in equal measure. I was terrified to speak; even more terrified of what would happen if I never did.

For the first time, I sat in a circle of women who didn't need me to explain the pain behind my jokes, my pauses, or my patterns; they already knew. Their stories weren't identical to mine, but they rhymed; different details, same ache. That was when it clicked that the deepest kind of loneliness isn't being alone; it's believing you're the only one carrying this.

In that room, I learned that humor wasn't just a shield; it could be a bridge. I learned that vulnerability didn't automatically lead to punishment; sometimes it led to connection. I learned that telling the truth doesn't make it heavier; it makes it something other people can help carry.

Saying the words out loud felt like exhaling after years of holding my breath. That room didn't fix everything; it wasn't magic or a cure. But it cracked the shell I'd been living inside; and that was enough to change the direction of my life.

That's where real healing started; not in being rescued or corrected, but in the quiet power of people who simply nodded and said, "Me too."

UNPACK

What has been harder for you—speaking your truth, or believing someone will care when they hear it?

_____

_____

_____

_____

What kind of support actually helps you heal—listening, humor, validation, touch, quiet presence, etc.?

_____

_____

_____

_____

TAKE CONTROL

Finish this sentence:

I used to believe healing had to happen alone, but now...

_____

_____

_____

_____

Now rewrite the rule:

I deserve support that feels...

_____

_____

_____

_____

WRITE IT OUT

- The first time I spoke my truth in front of others, I felt…
- Silence protected me once, but now…

Coulda Shoulda Been Adopted

Theme: Longing for Belonging

So here's something I don't always say out loud. Growing up, I used to fantasize about being adopted. Not in a movie way. I didn't want a new name or a bigger house or some magical rescue. I just wanted to belong somewhere that didn't feel so loud and tense all the time.

My mom used to tell me this story like it was a badge of honor; that my father wanted to put me up for adoption and she refused. She was proud of that. She'd say it like it proved something about her strength or love. And I'd nod along, because that's what you do. But inside, I was thinking, I kind of wish you had. Not because I didn't want to exist; but because I wanted a different place to land.

I used to imagine parents who looked at me the way other parents seemed to look at their kids; with softness instead of irritation, pride instead of pressure. I wondered what it would feel like to be chosen, instead of kept. To be wanted, not just accounted for.

The truth I didn't have words for back then was this: the family I needed didn't have to be the one I was born into.
This was the beginning of understanding that if I didn't belong where I came from, I wasn't broken. It just meant I'd have to find, build, and choose belonging later.

UNPACK

Did you ever fantasize about having a different family, a different home, or a different version of love? What did that version give you that was missing?

_____

_____

_____

_____

Have you built, found, or chosen a family later in life? What made it feel real?

_____

_____

_____

_____

TAKE CONTROL

Finish this sentence:

I thought family had to be...

_____

_____

_____

_____

Now rewrite the rule:

Belonging feels like...

_____

_____

_____

_____

WRITE IT OUT

- I used to believe someone else had to choose me…
- The family I needed as a child would have…

A Maltese and Herpes

Theme: Humor in Humiliation

Okay, so not every chapter of my life is tender or tragic in a meaningful, growth-oriented way. Some of them are just a mess. This was one of those. The kind you only survive by eventually turning it into a story you can laugh about later.

Enter the loser real estate agent. I nicknamed him The Toad; it felt right immediately. He bred his Maltese dogs and, in what should have been my first very obvious red flag, he gave me a puppy. Her name was Lola. We kept her for her entire life. Unfortunately, she wasn't the only thing that stuck around.

At the time, I was making decisions based on attention and validation, not long-term planning or self-preservation. And then came the diagnosis. Herpes. A plot twist I did not see coming and absolutely did not order.

I had this completely unearned moral superiority about my own body, which is wild considering I also didn't protect myself. Biology does not care about your internal judgment system. I didn't protect myself, so I got infected. Full stop.

The real turning point was realizing I didn't have to keep choosing people who treated my body and my trust like they were disposable.

Lola stayed. The herpes did too. The lesson, thankfully, stuck hardest.

UNPACK

Have you ever had an experience that felt humiliating in the moment, but later became a source of strength, humor, or empowerment?

_____

_____

_____

_____

What did this chapter of your life teach you about self-worth, boundaries, or choosing partners?

_____

_____

_____

_____

TAKE CONTROL

Finish this sentence:

I used to think humiliation meant I was broken, but now…

_____

_____

_____

_____

Now rewrite the rule:

The truth is…

_____

_____

_____

_____

WRITE IT OUT

- If I don't laugh, I'll cry! Laughing is healing because…
- That moment didn't define me; what defined me was…"

Dating a REAL Prince

Theme: Healing Love

So then there's Chris. Yes, that Chris. Prince Chris, if we're being accurate. We met at speed dating, which already sounds like a punchline. Our first date was six months after our first meeting because, unfortunately, I was dating The Toad.

Nine months after our first date, Chris and I got married. And before anyone asks, no, I wasn't pregnant. We just knew. We were done. Neither of us had any interest in continuing to audition people or collect dating horror stories.

Dating Chris was the first time love didn't come with anxiety attached to it. No manipulation. No chaos. No punishment disguised as passion. He was kind. He was steady. There was room for me to just… be myself.

The real shift was that I had finally done enough healing to recognize what healthy looked like and not run from it. The relationship didn't fix me. It just showed me what was possible when I stopped confusing intensity with intimacy.

Sometimes the most healing love is the kind that quietly proves you weren't asking for too much. You were just asking the wrong people.

UNPACK

What parts of you softened when you no longer had to defend, perform, or prove yourself?

_____

_____

_____

_____

What did healthy love teach you about your future standards and self-worth?

_____

_____

_____

_____

TAKE CONTROL

Finish this sentence:

I used to think love meant surviving, but now I know...

_____

....

....

....

Now rewrite the rule:

The version of me learning how to receive love needed...

_____

....

....

....

WRITE IT OUT

- Being loved without fear felt like…
- I finally realized I should be treated with kindness…

Losing My Mom

Theme: Complicated Grieving

My mom died in 2019, and grief didn't arrive the way people like to describe it. There was no collapse, no flood of tears, no dramatic moment of realization. What showed up instead was paperwork, phone calls, and the quiet shock of knowing she was gone because someone else went to check on her when she stopped answering the phone.

I hadn't seen her in over a year. She refused help; refused to move closer; refused every offer meant to make her life safer or softer. She chose distance, independence, and control, even when it meant isolation. And now, six years later, I still haven't cried. I am grieving a mother who died, and I am also grieving a mother I never fully had.

What I carry isn't simple. There is sadness for what was lost, for what never existed, for the parts of her I loved and the parts of her I spent decades trying to outrun. There is guilt; the kind that quietly asks whether I could have done more, even when I know the answer. There is relief, too, because the struggle between us finally ended. I no longer brace myself for the next crisis, the next emotional storm, the next refusal of help.

Complicated grief is quiet. It lingers. It lives in unfinished stories, in love that never found a safe shape, in the question of how you mourn someone who was both the wound and the beginning. I am still learning how to hold the truth of a mother I could not save; and how to let go without losing myself.

UNPACK

Have you ever lost someone you loved but also struggled with — someone whose absence brings more than one emotion?

_____

_____

_____

_____

What do you wish you could have said — or heard — before the relationship ended?

_____

_____

_____

_____

TAKE CONTROL

Finish this sentence:

I thought grief had to look a certain way, but now I know...

_____

_____

_____

_____

Now rewrite the rule:

My grief is valid even when it feels...

_____

_____

_____

_____

WRITE IT OUT

- When this person died, I lost the possibility of...
- I am grieving the real person and the person I needed...

When the House is Quiet

Theme: Empty Nest

When Sergio moved to Orlando for school, the house changed overnight. I expected the quiet, but I didn't expect how disorienting it would feel to walk through rooms that suddenly had no urgency attached to them. I was proud of him and excited for what he was building, and at the same time aware that a chapter I had lived inside for years had ended. Then COVID happened and stretched that uncertainty even further.

Worry settled in differently with him being far away and the world felt unstable. There were days when the distance felt manageable and days when it felt enormous. Parenting doesn't stop when your child leaves home; it just becomes quieter and more internal, filled with checking in, trusting, and learning when to sit with the anxiety instead of acting on it.

Chris and I found ourselves recalibrating during that period. With fewer daily logistics to manage, our attention shifted back to each other. We had space to notice who we were becoming and what we wanted our life to look like next. There was grief tucked into that awareness, and also a sense of possibility that surprised me.

Moving to Phoenix grew out of that reckoning. A new place offered room to reset and to build routines that belonged to this stage of life. It didn't replace what we missed; it gave us forward momentum. I learned that you can carry longing and still make choices that feel hopeful and grounding.

UNPACK

Have you experienced empty nest syndrome or lived far away from a much loved friend or family member?

_____

_____

_____

_____

What do you remember from this time?

_____

_____

_____

_____

TAKE CONTROL

Finish this sentence:

Life didn't feel normal because...

_____

_____

_____

_____

Now rewrite the rule:

In my life today, I feel happiest when...

_____

_____

_____

_____

WRITE IT OUT

- If I could go back and talk to myself then...
- I focused on emptiness, and it cost me...

Extiguishing a Gaslighter

Theme: Reclaiming Memories after Self-Doubt

For a long time, I learned to doubt my own memory. My mom, Janet, had a way of telling stories that erased what I remembered feeling and living through. When I brought up hard moments, she'd smooth them over, revise them, or dismiss them entirely. She told me things never happened the way I remembered. Over time, that kind of rewriting doesn't just confuse you; it trains you to question yourself.

One of the clearest examples was how she talked about Rod. She insisted he helped us a lot. That he wasn't abusive. I was remembering things wrong or being dramatic. She framed him as a net positive in our lives, and by extension, framed my reactions as misplaced or ungrateful. Hearing that over and over created a quiet fracture between what I knew in my body and what I was being told was true.

Learning to trust my own memories again happened slowly, through therapy, reflection, and the uncomfortable act of saying, "I remember this differently," and not backing down. I began to understand that minimizing harm doesn't erase it; it just relocates it inside the person who lived through it. Trusting myself meant accepting that someone else's denial didn't invalidate my experience.

This became one of the most important shifts in my healing. I stopped needing my mother to confirm what I already knew.

UNPACK

When was the first time you were told a memory was wrong?

_____

_____

_____

_____

Which version of the story did you accept as truth?

_____

_____

_____

_____

TAKE CONTROL

Finish this sentence:

The memory I keep defending is...

_____

_____

_____

_____

Now rewrite the rule:

In my life today, I trust my perceptions because...

_____

_____

_____

_____

WRITE IT OUT

- Doubting myself kept me safe by…
- Trusting myself now looks like…

Hating the Mirror

Theme: Body Dysmorphia

I learned to talk about my body the way my mother did; out loud, critically, as if it were a public project instead of a private home. I didn't just notice flaws; I announced them. What needed fixing. What I'd change. Which surgery would solve which problem. It became so normal that I didn't realize how harsh it sounded until I caught myself saying it casually, like it was small talk.

My mom narrated her body constantly. Weight, skin, aging; everything was up for evaluation. I absorbed that language early and carried it forward without questioning it. Body dysmorphia shows up quietly in my life. In mirrors I avoid and mirrors I study too closely. In photos, I zoom in on and compliments I brush aside. It shows up in how quickly my mood can shift based on a reflection or a passing thought that still knows exactly where to land.

I have started being kinder to my body as it has carried me through fear, grief, illness, desire, pregnancy, parenting, and survival. It has held memory and emotion when words weren't available yet. My body doesn't require improvement before it earns respect. It has already done enough.

UNPACK

When did you become aware of how bodies were talked about?

_____

_____

_____

_____

Whose voice do you hear most clearly when you judge your body?

_____

_____

_____

_____

TAKE CONTROL

Finish this sentence:

I comment on my body most when...

_____

....

....

....

_____

Now rewrite the rule:

I have stopped hating my image because...

_____

....

....

....

_____

WRITE IT OUT

- **My body has carried me through...**
- **The positive words and tone I use now...**

WANNA SHARE YOUR STORY?

When you work with Lisa, you get:

- A story structure that works.
- A voice that sounds like you.
- Support through the messy middle of a project.
- Tools to push through perfectionism and self-doubt.
- Real feedback from a real writer who's been there.
- Supportive, judgment-free zone (with a healthy dose of humor).
- Personalized sessions to build your writing skills.

CONTACT ME FOR A FREE TWENTY-MINUTE CONSULTATION:

LISAGERARDYWRITER@GMAIL.COM

UNFILTERED THOUGHTS

_____
_____
_____
_____
_____
_____
_____
_____
_____
_____
_____
_____
_____
_____
_____
_____
_____

WORK IN PROGRESS

AN UNSENT LETTER

_____

_____

_____

_____

_____

_____

_____

_____

_____

_____

_____

_____

_____

_____

_____

_____

WHAT COMES NEXT

FIND ME ONLINE

If this workbook stirred something in you and you want to stay connected:. You can contact me at lisagerardy.com. There's a handy QR code below.

I also host the **Cracked Track Parenting** group on Facebook; a thoughtful, honest space for parents who are trying to do things differently and break old patterns.

You don't have to do this work alone.